Avoiding & Dealing with Offenses

Delilah Crowder

Avoiding & Dealing with Offenses

Published by
DPC Ministries Enterprises Inc.
All Right Reserved

©2013 por Delilah P. Crowder
Printed in the United States of America

Any part of this publication is not to be reproduced, processed on any system that can reproduce it or transmitted by any mechanical system such as electronics, copier, tape, or any other, except for short quotes with prior permission of the author.

All scripture quotations were taken from :the King James Version of the Bible unless otherwise noted.

ISBN-13: 978-0615878096
ISBN-10: 0615878091

Editing by Sherlin Shoffner Taylor | sherltay@aol.com

Cover design and interior: Karina Chavez
karina.chavez@jdh.org.ar

ACKNOWLEDGEMENTS

To my Lord and Savior Jesus Christ, thank you for Your eternal love that is poured into my heart and, for the revelation of your Word that takes me daily each day to live a life of seeking into you and your truths.

To my husband, Rev. Christopher Crowder, thank you for the sacrifices that you makedo, for spiritually covering me with prayer, and for going in front as the head and priest of our home.

And finally, to all the people who contributed to this book in any way, thank you for your inspiration, knowledge, and creativity.

Thank you so much,
Delilah Crowder

CONTENTS

Acknowledgements 5

Prologue 9

Introduction 11

Part I What is an offense? 15

Part II How do I know I am offended? 29

Part III How and when do offenses happen? 47

Part IV Dealing with the offenses 59

Part V Forgiveness 73

Part VI Devastating offenses 83

Final Words 91

Biography 93

PROLOGUE

Pastor Delilah Crowder is a teacher of the Word of God. Her life is a great example of a woman of faith and wisdom who loves the Lord.

In her new book, written from her heart, she develops the theme of offenses in a very particular way.

Throughout eternity, offenses have made many people lose the correct perspectives of their lives and their sense of being. The agony that generates in every one of them is greater when they don't have a guide that instructs them and sets them free of this horrible spiritual and emotional disease.

In each chapter of this work, you will find the key to winning this battle: the love of God. You will find that when you act through Him and you are filled with His presence, it is then that you are able to open your heart, forgive those who have offended you, and receive the soul healing that you need to reach the divine purposes for your life.

I invite you to join Pastor Delilah in AVOIDING AND DEALING WITH OFFENSES by immersing yourself in this experience that will transform your life.

Pastor Nixon Cruz
Iglesia Casa de Adoracion Jabes
Bayamon, Puerto Rico

INTRODUCTION

*The discretion of a man makes him slow to anger,
And his glory is to overlook a transgression.*
Proverbs 19:11

Offenses come into our lives through different circumstances, people, and ways; but there is something they all have in common. It is the impact that we receive when they come to us. They can be emotional, physical, and demoralizing hits and can affect our circumstances and quality of life.

The truth is that every day millions of people walk around carrying recent and longstanding offenses. Offenses are burdens that increasingly bind us like chains and keep us captive. They drown us and destroy us as years go by. This is something to which I can testify myself. Even though I was saved and working in the ministry, for many years I carried offenses that put me in an emotional prison. It wasn't until the Holy Spirit came to minister to me that I took responsibility for my feelings and had freedom. That freedom led me to start enjoying a life full of peace and blessings. Many people are captive in the prison of offenses and are their own jailers. They have the key in their hands to open the door of the prison, but because of pride or need for revenge, they remain tied up and cannot enjoy the freedom which Christ purchased on the cross of Calvary.

So that we may have a clear understanding of offenses, we need to keep in mind that in the act of offense, both the offender and the victim are participants. At some point we have found or we will find ourselves in both positions. There are aggressors that have come to our lives and left and some that are still there. There are aggressors that we can completely eliminate and there are others that, because of family ties, we must continue to see. In the latter case, we can only try to manage the relationship in a healthy and constructive way for both people.

Throughout my life, I have experienced a

multitude of offenses: daily and small offenses and big and devastating offenses (we will analyze both types of offenses in detail later). Each of these experiences have shaped me and helped to make me the person I am today.

Offenses have made me sensible, but they also have made me strong. At some point, they made me fall to the floor with both hands, but they also gave me the strength, inspiration and courage to stand on my feet and keep going.

Offenses always come to our lives whether we like it or not; even Jesus let us know in Luke 17:1 that they would always come, but it is our attitude towards them that will make the difference. You decide if you are going to become another statistic or a permanent victim or not. Only you can determine to learn from these circumstances and take strength to overcome them and continue your journey.

The purpose of this book is to share with you practical strategies that you can apply to your daily life in order to have better control when you are offended and to teach you the forms and characteristics of offenses so that you can eliminate the present ones and those that will come in the future.

Pastor Delilah
Crowder

PART 1

If the spirit of the ruler rises against you,
Do not leave your post;
For conciliation pacifies great offenses.
Ecclesiastes 10:4

WHAT IS AN OFFENSE?

First, an offense is generally an insult or some kind of treatment done to an individual, either directly or indirectly, that results in a personal hurt. This comes due to physical, sexual or emotional abuse. It can also be the result of a material loss, such as a job or home, or social, professional, or economic position. An offense can be small and insignificant or enormous and devastating.

An offense can occur when we feel insulted at work because, even though we have dedicated time and effort, we are fired for no reason. In this case, we perceive the loss of employment as unfair and are hurt and offended by this action.

We also feel offended when a business transaction, in which we had all our hope, fails or when we did not receive the expected promotion and a coworker was promoted instead of us.

An offense can take place when we lose our home, our automobile or our social and economic position due to divorce. This situation is common for women who suddenly find themselves alone, without a job and without any financial support.

We can feel insulted when our kids are not invited to a birthday party or to a special event that they have anxiously awaited or when the coach leaves them on the bench during the game and they don't get any playing time.

In the Bible we find an example in the book of Ruth. We learn about Naomi, Ruth's mother-in-law. After she lost her husband and her two sons, she returns to her homeland. When women come to visit her, she tells them not to call her Naomi any more, but to call her Mara which means bitterness (see Ruth 1:20).

In Ruth 1:20 we see that Naomi felt offended by God. Yes, you read right, by God! Even though it was the decision of Naomi and her husband to leave Israel, she blamed God for her tragedy. In the Word of God there is no divine indication of such decision. In the same way, we can find ourselves in circumstances that we, ourselves, provoked; however in a desperate attempt to alleviate our pain, we blame others for those circumstances, even God.

We tend to ask God:

• God, why have you abandoned me? Why not some one else?
• Why did my friend get a house with no effort, while I

am obedient and I'm doing what a Christian should do, and I don't have one?
- Is there something I'm doing wrong that doesn't allow me to have your favor, or your miracles?
- Why it is that her father was healed and not mine?
- Why don't you keep in mind the desires of my heart?
- Why don't you move your hand in my favor?
- Why aren't you doing anything?

And when we don't hear God, we say:
God does not hear me.
God does not take me into account.
He has forgotten me.

    And without knowing it, we have resentment, we get angry with God and everything hurts even more. But we forget that God is good, His mercies are renewed every morning, and even when we lose control of situations, He is still in control. We forget that everything we have is by His grace and that He is good. Instead, we are offended.

---

[1] Gary Chapma, El enojo, Como Manejar Una Emoción Poderosa de Una Manera Saludable, Editorial Portavoz, edición

In Judges 6:13, Gideon asks: *"...why then has all this happened to us? And where are all His miracles which our fathers told us about, saying, 'Did not the Lord bring us up from Egypt?' But now the LORD has forsaken us and delivered us into the hands of the Midianites."* Gideon's attitude clearly demonstrates to us his feelings of offense by God. His answer to God's angel was full of sarcasm.

In the same way, when we are going through trials and tribulations or we suffer disappointments, we consciously or unconsciously feel offended by God. Proof of this offense is the distance that we put between Him and us. All of a sudden we stop praying, we stop going to church, or we stop serving Him.

Theologically we know that God does not fail, but emotionally we get angry. When we look at Job and other biblical examples of people that got mad at God, it is clear that He did not condemn such anger. Rather, He entered into a dialog with these people and helped them to grow in the midst of their anger and overcome it. However, it does not mean that God will always give an explanation of why bad things happen to good people. The book of Job is a lengthy discourse between Job and his friends and between Job and God. His friends basically accused him of doing something wrong and insisted that the tragedy was God's judgment for his sin. Job told them again and again that this was not the case.

Job's definitive answer was to trust God, even if he didn't understand what was happening. Because of this experience and Job's faithfulness to trust God, the relationship between Job and God was strengthened and deepened. In chapter 42, you will see that "... *the Lord blessed the latter days of Job more than his beginning" (v 12).*

There are many people that feel offended by God. And even if they don't dare utter those feelings out loud, their behavior is crying out that they are offended by God. This is absolutely understandable when they are going through a period of intense pain. But since we were created to have an intimate relationship with the Lord, our pain intensifies when we are missing this relationship in our lives. He is on our side, and not against us!

Secondly we can define offense as a moral outrage or damage. This type of offense is connected to our emotions and it comes along with situations such as betrayal, abandonment and lies among other things.

Offense through moral damage comes when a husband leaves his wife for another woman after years of marriage; when a friend you trusted betrays you by telling the intimate secrets that were shared with them; or when a close relative does not offer support when needed the most.

The offense through outrage takes place when we are accused of something we didn't do or say, and as a result we lose our credibility to others; or when the person in whom we trusted the most leaves us in a difficult moment.

Other examples of offenses are the birthday cards that were never received, the call that was never made, the money we loaned that was never repaid, the false rumor that someone spread against us, or the missing gratitude for a favor we did for someone.

We can find an example of this in 1 Chronicles 15:29 where the Word tells us that Michal despised David when she saw him dancing in the presence of God. I dare say that she despised him not just because he was dancing. Michal's contempt comes from years of abandonment and waiting for David while he was in exile. Years full of uncertainty and pain during which no one stopped to ask her how she felt. She was treated as just a piece of property. Keep in mind that during David's exile, her father Saul gave her as a wife to another man and when David came back, he took her back without question, and without consideration. All of this probably resulted in resentment, contempt, and great psychological damage to her.

As you can see, daily offenses come from everywhere and in different ways. It doesn't matter where in the planet we live or in what situation of life we find ourselves. We are not exempt from offenses and we should not pay very close attention to them. If we give them importance and take them seriously, they can destroy our emotions and our interpersonal relationships.

TYPES OF OFFENSES

For the reader's benefit and for the purpose of analysis on this subject, we will summarize the offenses in two categories:
1. Daily offenses
2. Devastating offenses

Daily offenses are those that we face in our daily lives. For example, your child wasn't the goalie in the soccer game (the whole family was expecting it!); the cashier threw the change instead of putting it in your hand; you never received that text message from the expected person; and the ex-husband, for the umpteenth time, was not on time to pick up the kids.

A daily offense is one that suddenly occurs and you find yourself not talking to your friend. If someone asks you what happened or why aren't you talking to your friend, you respond by saying that you have no idea. You say she suddenly stopped calling me and even unfriended me on Facebook. I really don't know what happened. When these situations occur, they can be very disconcerting.

It's those little particles that fall into the milk, that grow little by little, until one day we lose our patience and explode. The more serious situations happen when we decide to call a friend to tell him or her everything they did to us, or even worse, post it on a social network site so that everyone knows!

We also face very devastating offenses, those that come through damages caused by physical, emotional and sexual abuse. These can be by the abandonment of your mother or father in childhood, by infidelity from your partner for whom you'd give everything, or by public defamation. These are damages that tear at our soul to the point that we feel we are dying because our world has crashed.

This kind of offense should be treated with major care. If we don't, we are risking losing the marvelous opportunity that God has given us to live victorious, prosperous and abundant lives.

What would you gain by insulting a stone that is incapable of hearing you? Well then, imitate the stone and don't listen to the insults that your enemies (or friends) send to you.[2]

Later in this book we will see these more closely, but for now we will concentrate on the daily or small offenses.

---

[2] Epicleto de frigia (55-135) Filoso grecolatino

ACTIVITY

Name five people who you feel have offended you and describe the cause of the offense.

1._____

_____

_____

_____

_____

2._____

_____

_____

_____

_____

3._____

_____

_____

_____

_____

4._____

_____

_____

_____

_____

5._____

_____
_____
_____
_____

As we read through these pages, we will work and incorporate these people and these situations.

PART 2

For if ye forgive men their trespasses, your heavenly Father will also forgive you.
Matthew 6:14

HOW DO I KNOW THAT I AM OFFENDED?

Many people tend to say that there is no offense in their lives. They say this because either they believe it or they refuse, consciously or unconsciously, to see the reality of their situation. The truth is that nearly everybody has some offense in their lives and there are certain signs that can indicate it.

In Ephesians 4:31-32, we read: *Let all bitterness, and wrath, and anger, and clamour, and evil speaking, be put away from you, with all malice: And be ye kind one to another, tenderhearted, forgiving one another, even as God for Christ's sake hath forgiven you.*

In this Bible passage we see one of the best descriptions of a sign that an offense exists. These are like thermometers that indicate to us if we are offended or not. Let's analyze each of them.

1. Bitterness

Bitterness comes through affliction and disgust. It is related to that bitter flavor that comes from very deep in the heart of a person. It is a resentment that sur-ges when they hear the mention of someone's name.

The first characteristic of bitterness is sarcasm (an example is what we saw in Gideon's life) that is hurtful irony, or even mockery. An example is when the children's father comes late to pick them up and, even though he apologizes and is demonstrating repentance, the ex-wife says, "If you really cared about the children, you'd be on time…."

In Genesis 30:14-15, we can see very clearly the bitterness that Leah felt against Rachel when Rachel asked her for her son's mandrakes. Leah answered, *"Is it a small matter that thou hast taken my husband? and wouldest thou take away my son's mandrakes also?…"*

The second characteristic of bitterness is agitation. An example of this type of bitterness is when you speak to someone and you find yourself upset and your emotions are not in order. When there is bitterness is our lives, there is no way to speak temperately (especially if you are Caribbean!). Every conversation, as simple as it can be, will rise up as the milk in the fire. This is one of the characteristics that I have experienced in the past and now that I have recognized it, I have been able to not only to work on it, but also to avoid it in my life.

The third characteristic of bitterness is projecting a false happiness. And of this one we all are guilty. As John 8:7 says, *"So when they continued asking him, he lifted up himself, and said unto them, He that is without sin among you, let him first cast a stone at her."* False happiness occurs when we constantly try to demonstrate to others that everything in our lives is marvelous and we only have triumphs. In reality, you are constantly competing with those around you, trying to impress them with the best car, the bigger house and the more exotic vacations. If someone else achieves triumph or success and you refuse to acknowledge it or congratulate them, that too is a sign of bitterness.

The fourth and last characteristic of bitterness is defamation. This is when you talk about others and speak negative and untrue things about them in an attempt to discredit them, either directly or with others. This happens mostly in casual and private conversations, sometimes over a cup of coffee. They are quick and innocent comments that are full of criticisms and prejudices, even though the Word gives us the commandment in Exodus 20:16 to not bear false witness against our neighbors.

I invite you to consciously examine your heart to determine if any of the characteristics of bitterness mentioned above are being manifested in your life in regards to one or more persons. If the answer is yes, this means that you have been offended by that person even if you are not consciously aware of it.

In 1 Samuel we find Saul pursuing David, without resting, to kill him. Saul lost the last years of his life immersed in hatred and bitterness. Jealousy and thoughts of murder and violence against David were consuming him. In his attempt to kill David, Saul wasted resources that belonged to the kingdom. He neglected the throne and many died as a result. Finally, Saul lost his soul. The same thing happens to us when we get obsessed with a moral or emotional persecution -- we waste years of our lives, resources and even our blessings.

Deuteronomy 29:18 tells us: *"Lest there should be among you man, or woman, or family, or tribe, whose heart turned away this day from the LORD, our God, to go and serve the gods of these nations; lest there should be among you a root that beareth gall and wormwood."* This is reminding us that like the tree, bitterness grows with roots that extend and take control not only of our emotions, but also those of our children, our partners, and the people we love.

Bitterness steals from us the resources we have and it stops us from receiving the blessings of God and all of those things that belong to us.

Many of us are witnesses to how some women, full of bitterness about an ended marriage, work to destroy their ex-husbands, and in the process, destroy their children and the relationships they have with them.

I want to share with you a part of my life story. During the first nine years of my life I was not privileged to live with my parents. I lived from house to house, from family to family. Tomorrow was always uncertain. And it was because my mother's heart was full of offense toward my father and she didn't allow my sister and me to spend time with him. She left us with other people to take care of us and during that process I was sexually violated and physically abused. All of this is the result of bitterness. I am very thankful to God that He has changed my mother. Now she has Christ in her heart and is delivered from all offense and the sad consequences of it in her life.

A root of bitterness is an act, a situation, or a memory that we are neither able to forget or forgive. We continue to give it importance, and as a result, it stops all the new and good things that may come later in life. Although the offense that caused the bitterness may have happened some time ago, a root of bitterness is a memory that still has the same effect as it did when it happened. The accusation, the betrayal, the infidelity, the insult, or the offense becomes our own internal enemy. It becomes an enemy, because the pain of that memory is keeping us in the past and comes against our peace. It clouds the present and it does not allow us to keep dreaming and continuing to our goals. And who gets hurt with a root of bitterness? You!! Most likely, the person that caused the offense doesn't even know of the pain you are enduring and yet you're still carrying something that can be left behind. Let it go so that it will no longer have authority and power over your life.

The root of bitterness doesn't only destroy our emotions, but also our mind and body. The apostle Paul says, *"Certainly there are things I have before me, everything I want to accomplish, but in order to accomplish it, to go to the future I have to let go of the past, otherwise, I will be always stuck in the same place."* Philippians 3:14 And the same happens to our lives.

It is very important that we create a habit of examining ourselves, and if necessary, to pull out every root of bitterness completely before we lose our blessings and destroy, with our own hands, our home, our children and our families.

It is the will of God for us to be free from all bitterness, and that freedom is accessible to each and every one of us today if we chose to change.

2. Wrath

Wrath comes with violence; it is like a

boiling heat in our guts. We can compare it to a pressure cooker which, little by little and according to the fire, starts to steam and make noise and then start shooting. Have you ever felt that way?

The most common characteristics of wrath are accelerated palpitations of the heart, sweating hands, and even sometimes, breathing difficulties. It is an emotional agitation, an uncontrolled passion that reflects in all areas of our body.

Wrath also reacts physically, such as physical violence against another, throwing objects, slamming doors or hanging up the phone loudly, ending a call.

Ephesians 4:26 tells us, *"Be ye angry, and sin not: let not the sun go down upon your wrath."* All of us will get angry at some point. It is inevitable because it is human nature. The Apostle Paul tells us that there is a law in our bodies that makes everyone, with no exception, end up doing the wrong thing even though we want to do well.

In Matthew 21:12-13 we read that Jesus *"... went into the temple of God, and cast out all them that sold and bought in the temple, and overthrew the tables of the moneychangers, and the seats of them that sold doves, and said unto them, It is written, My house shall be called the house of prayer; but ye have made it a den of thieves."* We see here that Jesus went into the temple and turned over the tables of the merchants. But keep in mind that the wrath that is written about in Ephesians 4 is not the same that we see in these two verses in Matthew.

The emotion that Jesus manifested was an indignant wrath, for not showing reverence to the temple and for disobedience to the Word of God. Something we could call today a "holy and righteous anger".

In Genesis we see that Cain had wrath issues. The problem wasn't that he got angry; the problem was that he stayed in that controlling emotion. In the end he murdered his brother Abel of whom he was jealous. Cain's case teaches us that if we don't learn to control our wrath, it will control us and we will open the door to sin.

For many years I suffered with constant wrath. I wouldn't stop hurting, offending and destroying those who were by my side. All wrath has a foundation. We must seek direction from the Holy Spirit to lead us to the root of that emotion so it can be dealt with.

In most cases, the root of our wrath is not in the other person but in us; therefore it is important to examine ourselves periodically.

It wasn't until I opened my heart and worked with my emotions that I was able to exercise control over them. Today, my wrath is mostly in control, although sometimes my indignation for a lack of excellence, integrity and professionalism reminds me that wrath is something I still battle constantly. How do you find yourself in this area?

3. Anger

The third sign that there is offense in our lives is anger. Anger is annoyance, outrage, and grievance.

There is a big difference between wrath and anger. Anger is more passive, unlike wrath which expresses itself openly. An angry person tends to keep the feeling internally without letting others know about it. It is possible that the attitude and the posture of an angry person changes, but in most cases it is not perceived by those around them unless that person expresses annoyance or anger. Wrath is violent; anger is passive.

Most of the time anger comes when we feel that we have been disrespected or that our rights have been violated.

It doesn't matter what you've been taught, felling angry is not something bad; On the contrary, if we don't let ourselves get angry, the negative emotions will start accumulating until one day we explode.

Anger is a feeling, a mood change, given by God as a response to injustice. In Numbers 14:18 the scripture reveals to us that God is *"longsuffering, and of great mercy."* It tells us that God is slow to wrath, but in the midst of this emotion,

He extends His mercy. Like Jesus, we need to practice this spiritual law and extend our mercy towards those that have offended us.

4. Yelling

The fourth characteristic of offense is yelling. This consists of raising your voice in an abnormal way involving wrath. Wrath and yelling generally go hand in hand. They are never alone; they are always together -- like good friends.

Something very common is parents yelling at their kids, especially when they feel like they have not been heard or respected. We also see this in many couples. They feel internally that they are not being comprehended, and believe that if they raise their voice, the other person will understand them better. The truth is that yelling produces the opposite effect.

Yelling also indicates emotional separation. When we are emotionally and physically close to each other, we don't yell, we whisper. You may not believe it, but in my marriage there is no yelling. I think it is because both my husband and I are communicators. As a result, we sit down, analyze the problem and find the root. Another reason we don't yell could be because my husband doesn't speak Spanish and even though I speak English, I am much more passionate in Spanish. If I yelled in Spanish, he wouldn't understand me.

And last, yelling is also used as a mechanism to take control of a situation. This happens a lot in insecure people who hide their insecurities through yelling and violence.

Yelling is an alarm that something is wrong, not just to the one that hears the yelling but also to the person yelling. So pay very close attention and find the more appropriate solution if you notice this happening a lot in your personal life.

5. Slander

The last and fifth characteristic of offense is slander. Slander occurs when we falsely attribute to other persons acts that are not true, or when we do not have any evidence. It is easy to identify slander because we can hear it in phrases like "I think", "I believe", "I imagine": "I think that he doesn't love you", "I believe that she is ignoring you", "I think he's going to be late, as usual".

The purpose and outcome of slander is to bear false witness and defame the other person, damaging his or her reputation. We often see this in divorced couples where the father or mother assumes the reason for each other's actions in front of their children. For example, someone may say, "I think your mom sent you here so that she can get rid of you," when there is no evidence of such. One of the Ten Commandments in Exodus 20, tells us not to bear false witness.

Have you identified with one or more of the aforementioned characteristics? If so, keep reading. We will learn how to deal with and avoid these offenses. Later on this book, we will examine how to confront each of these characteristics in our lives.

ACTIVITY

The following are characteristics, feelings, and actions that you might recognize in your own life. Under each characteristic, write down the name of the person that causes you to feel or act this way. These should be the same names that you wrote during the last activity.

Bitterness _____
_____
_____
_____
_____

Wrath._____
_____
_____
_____
_____

Anger. _____
_____
_____
_____
_____

Yelling. _____

_____
_____
_____
_____

Slander _____

_____
_____
_____
_____

PART 3

But if ye forgive not men their trespasses, neither will your Father forgive your trespasses.
Matthew 6:15

HOW AND WHEN DO OFFENSES OCCUR?

Now that we have identified the characteristics of offense, we will now see how and when they can occur. This way, we will be adding to our arsenal of ammunition of ways to eliminate them and avoid them in our lives.

Unsatisfied Expectations

Offenses take place when our expectations are not satisfied. In Charles Dickens book, Great Expectations, we read the story of Miss Havisham. On the day of her wedding, her fiancé leaves her at the altar and disappears, taking a great deal of her fortune with him. From that moment, she demands that all the clocks of the house be stopped at the exact time she was left at the altar, and lives for the rest of her life wearing her wedding dress.

Miss Havisham had great expectations, not just from her fiancé, but also from life. She expected to live her life as a wealthy married woman. When this devastating event happened, besides being traumatized, Miss Havisham decides to avenger disappointment by damaging her peers. She adopts a beautiful young woman. In a malevolent form, she makes boys fall in love with the young woman and then separates them. The unfulfilled expectations of Miss Havisham motivated her to destroy the hearts of others, and kept her captive until the day of her death.

Like one of the main characters of this classic work, many of our offenses come into our lives as a result of what we are expecting to happen. For example, for your birthday you worked hard to prepare the invitations for your party and give them out on time. You decorated the house, prepared the food, and finally the day comes and everyone arrives for the party. Everyone enjoys themselves and leaves, leaving you with a messy house. And you find yourself extremely offended! When in reality, you did not ask for help to clean and organize the house after the party.

Another example of life not meeting your expectations is when you tell your teenaged children to clean and organize their rooms. When you return home, you find everything in the same place as it was when you left. You start yelling, offended because you feel they have disrespected you. When, in reality, you did not specify when you wanted the rooms to be cleaned. And, let's be honest, with teens we have to be very clear!

Now, if we examine this situation very closely, we find that the offense was not because of the mess, but because of the disrespect, devaluation and possibly other frustrations that you already had, like a hard day at work. Plus, you were possibly expecting something you have not taught your children: organization.

The same thing happens when you give expensive presents to your family for Christmas, birthday or other actions, and in return you receive a simple "Merry Christmas" or "happy birthday." The offense came because you were expecting something of similar value from the other person that never happened. You established those expectations yourself and ended up being you offended.

Again and again we feel offended by small things like the incident with the cashier at the supermarket, the waiting at the doctor's office, the email that took too long to receive a reply. When, in reality, each of these offenses could have been controlled or avoided if you would simply change your level of expectation.

Please understand that it is good to have expectations and to demand respect from others; but if you know that you will wait at the doctor's office, or there are going to be long lines at the supermarket, change your expectation or change to another doctor or another supermarket!

If we take time to evaluate each situation and establish realistic levels of expectation, we will eliminate and avoid many offenses in our lives.

Miscommunication

Another reason that we are offended is because of miscommunication. Communication consists of transmitting, notifying and exchanging information. When we don't transmit exactly what we want, the other person doesn't have a clear idea of what we are expecting. This causes miscommunication. When we miscommunicate our desires to another and our expectations are not met, we are offended. Those offenses take place because of our own miscommunication.

In the case of the doctor's office, it is necessary for you to be very clear, in a respectful way, of the kind of service you are expecting. The same applies if you give permission to your teenager to go to the shopping center. If you are not specific on the time your child should return home, you should not be offended if they do not return when you expect because you did not communicate clearly. If you enter into a business relationship, be clear with your partner. Clarity of communication is clear in order to avoid offense. Be clear with your friend, spouse, children, family members and others in your life. If we learn to communicate clearly what we expect from others, we will avoid hundreds of offenses and fewer relationships will be destroyed.

In the corporate world, companies offer an orientation day for new employees. During this orientation, the company's rules, procedures, and benefits are shared. They are very specific about what they expect from employees. If we don't comply with these rules and procedures, the company has the right to fire us. Therefore, we should not be offended if we find ourselves in this position, because the company clearly communicated their expectations to us.

Be clear, communicate well what you are expecting, and you will eliminate many offenses in your life.

Low Self-esteem

People with low Self-esteem are easily offended. Self-esteem is the value we give to ourselves, the appreciation and consideration that we feel about ourselves. This valuation doesn't always come from our attributes and triumphs, but by recognizing who we are as individuals in the body of Christ.

The person with low self-esteem tends to seek valuation and acceptance from others; when this doesn't happen, he or she is offended. The lack of self-identity -- not knowing who he or she is and what his or her purpose in life is -- makes that person desperately long for external approbation and, every time it is not received, feel emotionally wounded.

This was the case of Naaman in 2 Kings 5. He was offended when the prophet didn't come to receive him. Instead, the prophet sent his servant with a message. Even though Naaman was an army general, he was hungry for valuation and acceptance from others because he had low self esteem.

The person with low self-esteem tends to get offended frequently and easily. They assume or conclude what others' attitudes, thoughts, and feelings are and then slanders others. Slander is always the result of low self-esteem.

As with our previous scenarios, the offended person assumes that their text or email was not answered because the other person didn't want to answer, instead of assuming that it was a technical glitch and the message or email was not delivered.

The person with low self-esteem lives with a constant paranoia that will not allow him or her see the clear reality of things. Once offended (with or without any reason), he or she, like Miss Havisham, will offend and hurt others in retaliation.

Loss of Control

Lastly, offenses come when we feel like we

have lost control of a situation. When we have control, we have dominion and authority, and we enjoy the peace of independence and freedom.

In Genesis 1:26-27 we see that God has created us in His image and likeness with the attributes to rule and have dominion and authority. For this reason when we lose control of some areas in our lives, we are offended.

When there is physical, sexual, or emotional abuse, you lose control at that very moment, and feel you have no control of the situation and circumstances. This results in feelings of impotence, which causes the offense to multiply, and makes it even more devastating.

Another example of unmet expectations is when there is adultery in a marriage. First, the expectations are broken and the betrayed spouse feels like they have lost control.

When we lose control, wrath, anger, bitterness, and yelling occur. In those instances, all of the characteristics of offenses are manifested.

A Chain Reaction

If we put together everything we have discussed so far, we will see that it is like a chain. We see that because of one's low self-esteem, he or she has high expectations of others, which are not clearly communicated. Now that person loses control or dominion of a situation, which produces anger, wrath, yelling, bitterness and slander.

ACTIVITY

In the next exercise, write the events that you listed in Part 1, this time giving a reason for the offense.

Unsatisfied Expectations

_____
_____
_____
_____
_____

Miscommunication

_____
_____
_____
_____
_____

Low self-esteem

_____
_____
_____
_____
_____

Loss of Control

_____
_____
_____
_____
_____

At this point in the exercises, you should have already determined which of these offenses have base and are ready to work on them.

PART 4

*And herein do I exercise myself,
to have always a conscience void
to offence toward God, and toward men.*
Acts 24:16

DEALING WITH OFFENSES

In the previous chapters we defined what an offense is. We saw each of its characteristics and how they come to our lives. Now that we have a clearer understanding and are able to identify some personal offenses, let's take responsibility for our emotions and work to remove those offenses from our lives once and for all.

In Ephesians 4:31-32 we read, *"Let all bitterness, wrath, anger, clamor, and evil speaking be put away from you, with all malice. And be ye kind to one another, tenderhearted, forgiving one another, even as God in Christ's sake hath forgiven you."* The first thing we need to do with our offenses is to forgive. Forgiving consists of tolerating, comprehending, having compassion and freeing the other person of guilt.

In the Apostle Paul's letter to the church at Ephesus, we are told to "abandon." This means to cease from maintaining, practicing, or using. We are called to get rid of the feelings, but to do so in the spirit of freedom, meaning by choice and without resentment or revenge. Every time we are offended (and we will be as long as we live), we have the freedom to choose how we are going to react. Are we going to hold a grudge and want to do evil for evil, or we are going to resist anger and forgive?

Some people express that they have been wounded in such a way that they find it impossible to forgive. Let me tell you that forgiveness does not consist of feelings, but in choosing to let go of the offense and the offender, which as a result will bring freedom. Whether we feel it or not, we all are able to forgive because we have the Holy Spirit that lives in us and He empowers us to do it.

Let's now see four steps to follow so that we can reach this objective.

1. Begin with yourself

In Mathew 22 we are called to love our neighbor as we love ourselves. So to love others, we first have to love ourselves. This is not pride or arrogance, but a fundamental requirement that we are called to do.

This love for ourselves is developed and grows as we work together with the Spirit of God and come to the knowledge of who we are and how God sees us. This process is long and can seem to be very painful for someone who has been a victim of abuse, but it is necessary so that we are able to love ourselves in a healthy and balanced way.

And we cannot love God without loving ourselves. Keep in mind that it is so important love ourselves that Jesus, in Matthew 22:37-40, said *"...thou shalt love the Lord thy God with all thy heart, and with all thy soul, and with all thy mind. This is the first and great commandment. And the second is like unto it, Thou shalt love thy neighbour as thyself. On these two commandments hang all the law and the prophets."*

King Solomon, the author of the Proverbs said, *"above all things guard your heart for it is the wellspring of life."* All of our feelings and emotions emanate from our hearts. It is in our heart where our dreams are born, our purpose in life, and the desire to fight. It is in our heart where we find reason to triumph and where we love, but also where we hate.

This is why we have to take care of our heart and pay attention to it. It is time to work on ourselves -- to discover why we act and react the way we do and to go in and uproot bitterness, anger, wrath, yelling and slander. Do you dare to do it? I assure you that it is worth the effort.

2. Discard wrath, anger and yelling

Wrath, anger and yelling are very intense passions and emotions that start with frustration and can end with severe fury. This can endure for as little as a few seconds or l as long as years. Even though we don't notice, there are people that live all of their lives with an intense repressed anger. To have these feelings is not a sin, as we mentioned at the beginning of this book; it is what we do with those feelings that can take us to sin.

Each and every one of us reacts with wrath, anger or yelling when we perceive that we are being treated unfairly, we have been damaged have been offended.

We can eliminate and avoid these feelings first by identifying what is provoking these feelings in our lives. Once we have identified it, we need to stay away until we have learned to control our wrath, anger and yelling.

If talking to your former partner provokes you to yell, it would be wise that you avoid their phone calls and find another way to communicate, such as through text messages and email.

Remember that the only person that you can control is YOU!!

One of the persons that abused me during my formative years is still a close part of my life. And even though I forgave her and there is no more physical abuse, this person continues to bring emotional abuse to my life. I believe she does so unconsciously because there has not been a complete emotional healing in her life. Even though it took me a long time to understand and comprehend, I learned that I can only change myself, and, therefore, I put boundaries of communication between us.

Although my Latin culture teaches differently, it leads us to put others before ourselves as a sign of humility. I let myself be governed by the Word of God which tells me that I should love myself first; and that if my brother (or sister) offends me, I must call him aside and have witnesses, but if he persists in the same argument, I must put separation between him and me. This is a way of respecting and taking care of ourselves.

Keep in mind that even though God calls us to forgive seventy times seven in a day (this is equal to four hundred and ninety times daily), He does not ask us to live under abuse ever!

The second step to controlling wrath, anger and yelling is to take a break away from the person or the situation. It is also recommended to have someone you trust to whom you can go to moments like this, a person that can give you healthy advice, such as a spiritual leader, a pastor or a counselor.

Lastly and most importantly, go to God in prayer and in sincerity, seeking Him for help and guidance on the matter.

3. Discard the Slander

A slanderer reveals or sensationalizes the private information of another or makes up falsehoods and lies about another. The slanderer is a gossip who hurls malicious and hurtful comments to harm another's reputation. Slander reveals very clearly the emotional state of the slanderer and of his or her low level of self-esteem. By degrading someone, the slanderer feels superior to the one they have slandered.

In Genesis 3 we find Satan raising up slander against God. And now he continues to do the same thing with us, whispering falsehoods in our hearts.

According to Exodus 20:16, slander is a sin. One of the Ten Commandments is, *"Thou shalt not bear false witness against thou neighbour."*

The first thing we have to do to get rid of slander is to recognize it, repent and seek forgiveness from God. Once we have done this, ask God for strength so that we won't fall into the same thing.

Secondly, in order to rid ourselves of the need to slander, we have to find the root and our intention behind it. We already know that one of the reasons we slander is because we are offended and hurt. By analyzing the root and intention behind our slander from a different perspective, we are more likely to be able to see the reason for it.

Thirdly, and this applies to every area, seek professional counseling of a leader or a pastor. A neutral person that is not directly involved in the situation will be able to give you much more practical advice more objectively.

And lastly, and this is directed especially towards women, remain silent!

Proverbs 10:19 says: *In the multitude of words there wanteth not sin: but he that refraineth his lips is wise.* If you do not have control of your words, stay away from people and circumstances that lead you to slander.

4. Discard Bitterness

In Genesis we find the story of Esau and Jacob, and learn that Jacob stole the blessing of his birthright from his brother. This was enough reason for Esau to let a bitterness root grow against Jacob during the years they were separated. Nevertheless, we find Esau, in chapter 33, embracing and kissing his brother when they meet after a long absence.

Life brings us situations which create in us feelings that we have been robbed of what was rightly ours -- things such as our rights, possessions and material goods. Circumstances such as these can create roots of bitterness in our hearts without us even realizing it. Regardless, we must work to rid ourselves of and uproot this very destructive feeling.

First, we can discard bitterness if we decide to recognize that there is a root of bitterness in our lives. This doesn't necessarily need to be public, but it is essential to achieve total freedom. Remember that you cannot overcome what you have not first recognized. In order to change, we need to be conscious of the fact that we need to change.

Secondly, and this can be difficult for some people, we have to forgive those who have hurt us or have done evil to us (in the next part of this book we will analyze the theme of forgiveness in more detail).

Lastly, we must be satisfied with what we have. In the gospel of Luke, Chapter 15, we find the oldest son of the house full of resentment and bitterness because of dissatisfaction in his life. He had everything. But despite this, he was focused on what had been granted to his brother who had done nothing but squander his paternal inheritance.

Likewise, it may not occur to you that bitterness does not let you see the blessings that you have in your hands. I encourage you to focus on all the good things that the Lord has poured down on you and those around you, and not on your shortcomings and difficulties.

When Paul was suddenly imprisoned in Rome, he had every right to be bitter. His brothers had abandoned him. He could have wondered where was God in all of this. Instead, he took advantage of the opportunity to preach the gospel of Jesus Christ to the Roman soldiers and did not allow bitterness in his life.

Casting Out All Legalism

In Matthew 7:3 we are asked, *"Why do you look at the speck of sawdust in your brother's eye and pay no attention to the plank in your own eye?"* In other words, what about you; what role did you play in the matter? As my father in law often says, "There are three versions: His side, her side and the truth." Or do you want to wash your hands like Pilate did and take no responsibility for your actions?

In the drama of your life, you played the leading role. I am not referring to situations in which you were abused or mistreated, but to your involvement in other situations in which you added your two cents.

We all do it. Or do you consider yourself the good guy? If so, your role has been to not take responsibility for your own life, but to play the victim. There are some situations that we could not help, but there were others in which we were totally or at least partially responsible.

So, it is time for us to take responsibility and recognize our part in the matter. If we do so, we will be able to avoid and eliminate offenses in our lives forever.

ACTIVITY

Review the events you listed in Part 1 and record how you were involved in each incident.

1._____
_____
_____
_____
_____

2._____
_____
_____
_____
_____

3._____
_____
_____
_____
_____

4._____
_____
_____
_____
_____

5. _____
_____
_____
_____
_____

PART 5

Confess your trespasses to one another.
James 5:16

FORGIVENESS: WHAT IT IS AND WHAT IT IS NOT?

Forgiveness occurs when we decide to change and transform our feelings. Forgiveness does not mean that we are declaring that no harm has been done to us and that such an action is acceptable. Forgiveness does not diminish the damage that was done to us and it is not a denial that an assault has occurred. Forgiveness does eliminate the consequences that the other person has to face because of their actions or sin.

The key is to "consciously decide," to let go of those feelings so that they will not continue to hurt us in the future. It is about letting go of the desire to hurt in return or to seek vengeance to cancel the debt of the other person. It is a difficult and uncomfortable process for some individuals more than others, depending on the degree of injury, but with God's help and guidance counselors and leaders, we can complete the process.

When we make the decision to forgive, God gives us the grace and strength to do it and to continue to have that attitude. Forgiveness does not show weakness but is one of the most powerful and valuable acts that we carry out in our lives. It takes courage to forgive.

Lack of forgiveness includes resentment, bitterness, hatred, hostility, anger, fear and stress toward a person who attacked us in some way. It is like a cancer that will consume your soul. By refusing to forgive, we are giving Satan license to continue hurting us. Forgiveness destroys the destructive power of the devil in our lives.

Reconciliation vs. Forgiveness

Forgiveness does not guarantee reconciliation. For this to happen, it takes two people, while forgiveness only requires one person, YOU. In 2 Samuel 14:33 we read that despite the attempt of David to reconcile with Absalom, there was no repentance or change of heart in Absalom and he eventually tried to take the throne of his father David (see 2 Samuel 15).

Forgiveness does not depend on the actions of the other person, or of a condition of probation. For example, someone may say, "I forgive you as long as you stop acting that way." Forgiveness does not require us to be humiliated or to allow the offender to continue hurting us. This is something we should be very clear on; otherwise, we may continue to be victims of guilt or manipulation and allow ourselves to be abused again.

Forgiveness is a gift you are giving to the other person. The trust must be regained and it is highly recommended that initially you set limits, rules and, in some cases, distance as already mentioned, until trust has been reestablished.

Do not expect the other person to repent in order for you to forgive. I repeat again that forgiveness is a gift to the offender and to you. When we forgive we are trusting God to take control, not only of the subject matter, but also of ourselves and our hurt feelings.

To forgive is to put ourselves in the other person's place, to humbly recognize in the Spirit our own weaknesses and sinful nature, and to be thankful that God first forgave us through Jesus Christ and His work on the cross of Calvary. That should already be enough reason to forgive, especially when it is difficult to do.

Reasons to forgive

The first reason to forgive is that forgiveness sets us free to get on with our lives. Remember that lack of forgiveness brings resentment, hatred, bitterness and these feelings can lead us to an emotional captivity that can end up destroying other relationships in our lives.

The second reason to forgive is to take the power and control from the other person over your life. When you do not forgive, you're giving up control, whether you like it or not. Lack of forgiveness does not hurt the offender. Instead, it hurts you.

Finally, we must forgive because if we do not, we are taking the risk of becoming bitter. Forgiveness protects us so that we will not become like the person who hurt us.

God and forgiveness

In Mark 11:26 Jesus said, *"But if you do not forgive, neither will your Father in heaven forgive your trespasses."* In other words, forgiveness from God is related to the way we forgive others.

When others offend us, let us remember how great is the mercy and forgiveness of God for us. If we refuse to forgive others, we are showing that we have no appreciation for the forgiveness we have received from the Lord.

Through the parable of the lost sheep, found in Matthew 18:21-35, Jesus clearly describes forgiveness and love. He exhorts us to reconcile and tells us that forgiveness should have no limits.

Often forgiveness is characterized as a Christian duty, however, this should not be done out of duty but out of love.

The desire for revenge can be so powerful that only God's love can fight it. In Genesis 45, we find the wonderful story of the time Joseph makes himself known to his brothers, who had sold him into captivity. Joseph had been separated from his family for years due to jealousy and resentment. This gives us a powerful lesson on how to forgive. One should forgive through a demonstrative love, despite the insults and injuries, and not by downplaying what happened.

Keeping forgiveness

When the guilt of our past sins come to torture us, we remember what God says through the prophet Isaiah in Isaiah 43:25, *"I, even I, am He who blots out your transgressions for My own sake; And I will not remember your sins."* So we, in like manner, not only forgive but forget and not bring to mind the transgression any more.

We must maintain the forgiveness even when doubt arises.

Remember, forgiveness is a choice, not a feeling. It consists of loving ourselves and being determined every day to keep completely free of hatred, resentment or bitterness by living the life of purpose to which each of us has been called.

ACTIVITY

Write the name of each person mentioned in the Part 1 and take the time to forgive them, either in person or in writing.

1._____
_____
_____
_____
_____

2._____
_____
_____
_____
_____

3._____
_____
_____
_____
_____

4._____
_____
_____
_____
_____

5. _____
_____
_____
_____
_____

PART 6

DEVASTATING OFFENSES

Included among devastating offenses are:

- *Sexual, verbal and emotional abuse,*
- *Physical and mental abuse, and*
- *Religious or spiritual abuse.*

The abuse issue has been taboo until now. Fortunately, today many men and women are finding the courage to speak out and bring information to others about their abuse and, in this way, face these horrific acts head on.

Experts tell us that between 10 and 20% of people have experienced some form of abuse. Just think, in a group of 500 people, about 100 of them may have suffered some form of abuse. At a youth meeting of 20 delegates, two or more have been abused. In an office of 50 employees, five have been victims of any of the above forms of abuse. And what's even worse, it may be that among this number, some of them are being abused right now.

These alarming figures indicate that every day, millions of people live their lives through the lens of abuse. That is why every day we see more and more dysfunctional families, who have problems moving forward in life. Many are immersed in alcohol, drugs and all kinds of addiction that promise to silence the voices that torment them daily.

When you are filled with hatred, bitterness, low self-esteem and in some cases sexual difficulties, hinder your ability to maintain any kind of healthy relationship with others. Most victims of abuse cannot live normal lives unless they receive professional and spiritual help.

Being abused is to be touched by the evil one. This brings shocking consequences. The degree of impact varies from case to case and from person to person, depending on the type of abuse, relationship to the perpetrator and the duration of such abuse. Likewise, abuse damages our emotions, bringing pain, anger, fear and guilt that can govern our lives completely.

Abuse is so great and deep an impact that it also damages the spirit of the person, affecting his or her ability and way of relating to God. This, many times, robs a person's hope and creates distrust in others, including God.

Keep in mind that the prophet Habakkuk tells us that, *"The just shall live by his faith."* Habakkuk 2:4. It is the individual's faith that brings him closer to God, promotes fellowship with Him and allows us to walk in God's promises. If a person, because of abuse, has developed distrust in others and has lost hope, they will, as a result, have difficulty in their walk as a believer.

Every leader needs to have knowledge of this information when working with people. In a

Christian environment we tend to try to solve everything with prayer. Although prayer is one of the most powerful weapons of the believer and should be our first resource, in order to take such individuals to a point where they can achieve a level of healthy faith, we may need to seek out other resources, media, and processes.

I am not speaking from a theoretical point of view but from experience. As mentioned earlier, I was repeatedly sexually molested. In addition, from the ages of 9 to 15, I was abused physically, verbally and emotionally daily. Finally, I experienced spiritual and religious abuse.

The road to recovery has been long and painful, and there were times when I fainted, but the indescribable love of God and the saving grace of our Lord Jesus healed, restored and completely transformed me.

Today I am able to declare in the words of Psalm 16:6, *"The lines are fallen unto me in pleasant places; yea, I have a goodly heritage."* It was through the guidance of the Holy Spirit and spiritual leaders and advisors, along with much prayer and fasting, that I was able to achieve this freedom.

What to do with devastating offenses?

The first step we must take is to confront and admit the reality of the events that happened to us. Denial is a defense mechanism of the mind which is to address the problem by denying its existence, because deep in our soul we want it not to be real. But the longer we deny reality, the more internal distress grows, stopping our growth and creating barriers for God to work in us.

The psalmist in Psalm 32:3 declares, *"When I kept silent, my bones waxed old through my roaring all the day long."* Silence consumed him day and night. In the same way, there are individuals who are consumed by silence and do not allow themselves to live lives that are victoious and fruitful.

God extends his hand. Open your heart to Him and receive the abundant life promised in His Word. For many years, I kept silent about my abuse and it was not until I started talking openly about it, and to work on myself with the right help, that inner healing came into my life.

Second, we must give ourselves permission to mourn. Emotions were given by God, I call them "thermometers" that indicate the condition our hearts. Give yourself permission to feel the pain and the damage that has come as a result of the abuse you have received. It's your right!

Third, we must fully depend on and surrender to God to reach health and recovery. One of my favorite scriptures is found in John 10:10 *The thief cometh not, but for to steal, and to kill, and to destroy: I am come that they might have life, and that they might have it more abundantly.* For many years I was robbed of that abundant life, but I thank God that today I can say I'm walking in the abundance of peace and love.

The fourth step to follow with devastating offenses is to seek help from professionals and others who specialize in that area. These people are experienced and will guide you into a healthy way of life so that you can deal with the abuse and triumph over it.

Finally, and I never tire of repeating this, it is essential to forgive. Remember that lack of forgiveness fills us with resentment, bitterness, hatred, hostility, anger and fear. It is like a cancer that consumes your soul. You and I have been especially designed and created to live a life that leads us daily from triumph to triumph. Do you dare take what is yours?

FINAL WORDS

Before finishing this book, I want you to know that God sent me to announce that this is your time of salvation and deliverance. If you are sad, know that there is consolation in God; He is willing to change your mourning into dancing and fill your life with victory. Do not worry about those who hurt you, do not seek your own revenge, because vengeance belongs to the Lord. He promises to repay you double with life filling blessings for what you went through.

I pray that the words of this book will help you get to that place.

BIOGRAPHY

Author and Pastor Delilah Crowder is originally from Bayamon, Puerto Rico. She came to the Lord as a teenager and has been preaching and teaching the Word of God for 27 years. She has studied Biblical Theology, Christian Counselling and Business Administration and is a certified Life and Ministry Coach.

She moved to the United States in the 1990's, and throughout her evangelistic and missionary work has established 12 churches on the East Coast of the United States. These churches have expanded throughout the Central and Western United States, Mexico and Central America.

In the last six years, together with Asesor Ministerial Inc., a non-profit organization, she has contributed as a church and ministry consultant for more than 250 Hispanic pastors, ministries and churches throughout the United States.

Pastor Delilah Crowder currently lives with her husband, Rev. Christopher Crowder in the Atlanta, Georgia area.

AUTHOR'S OTHER WORKS

CONTACT DETAILS

For speaking engagements and products,
visit our website:
www.delilahcrowder.com

www.ingramcontent.com/pod-product-compliance
Lightning Source LLC
Chambersburg PA
CBHW060846050426
42453CB00008B/864